NEW YORK CITY

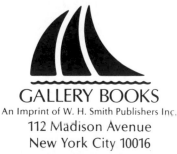

GALLERY BOOKS
An Imprint of W. H. Smith Publishers Inc.
112 Madison Avenue
New York City 10016

This edition first published in U.S.
in 1990 by Gallery Books,
an imprint of W.H. Smith Publishers, Inc.
112 Madison Avenue, New York, New York 10016

ISBN 0-8317-8826-7

Printed and bound in Spain

For rights information about the photographs in
this book please contact:

The Image Bank
111 Fifth Avenue, New York, NY 10003

Producer: Solomon M. Skolnick
Author: Moira Duggan
Design Concept: Leslie Ehlers
Designer: Ann-Louise Lipman
Editor: Madelyn Larsen
Production: Valerie Zars
Photo Researcher: Edward Douglas
Design Assistant: Kristi Jo McKnight
Assistant Photo Researcher: Robert Hale

Title page: *Thousands of runners cross the Verrazano-Narrows Bridge at the start of the New York Marathon, held yearly in October.* Above: *Panorama at sunset, with Circle Line sightseeing boat heading toward her pier on the Hudson River.*

Any living city is a center of dynamic human activity, a theater of operations for people of countless occupations—artists, artisans, bankers, chefs, doctors, journalists, lawyers, and zookeepers—to name a few. A city is a showcase for the powerful and assured, a springboard for the hopeful and ambitious, a shelter (of sorts) for the landless and oppressed. Planners and designers may be able to improve a city, but they cannot dictate where or when it will expand, decline, or change character. Such changes depend on things going on outside the city limits—on social and political events, on cultural ferment, on world markets.

All the forces that go into the making of a city have worked at top speed in the making of New York City. One of the youngest of the world's great cities—it received its first official name, Nieuw Amsterdam, in 1625—it is also one of the largest in terms of population. The astounding towers of Manhattan, visible from miles away, arise from a sliver of real estate about 2.5 miles wide and 12.5 miles long. In this comparatively small area, ringed by water, this "City of Cities" has virtually exploded into being. There are cities more beautiful than New York, many with longer and richer traditions, and some with cultural

This page and opposite: *Liberty has held her gleaming torch high since 1886, symbolizing hope and welcome to millions. A gift of the people of France, the statue stands on a small island in Upper New York Bay in view of the office towers of Lower Manhattan.*

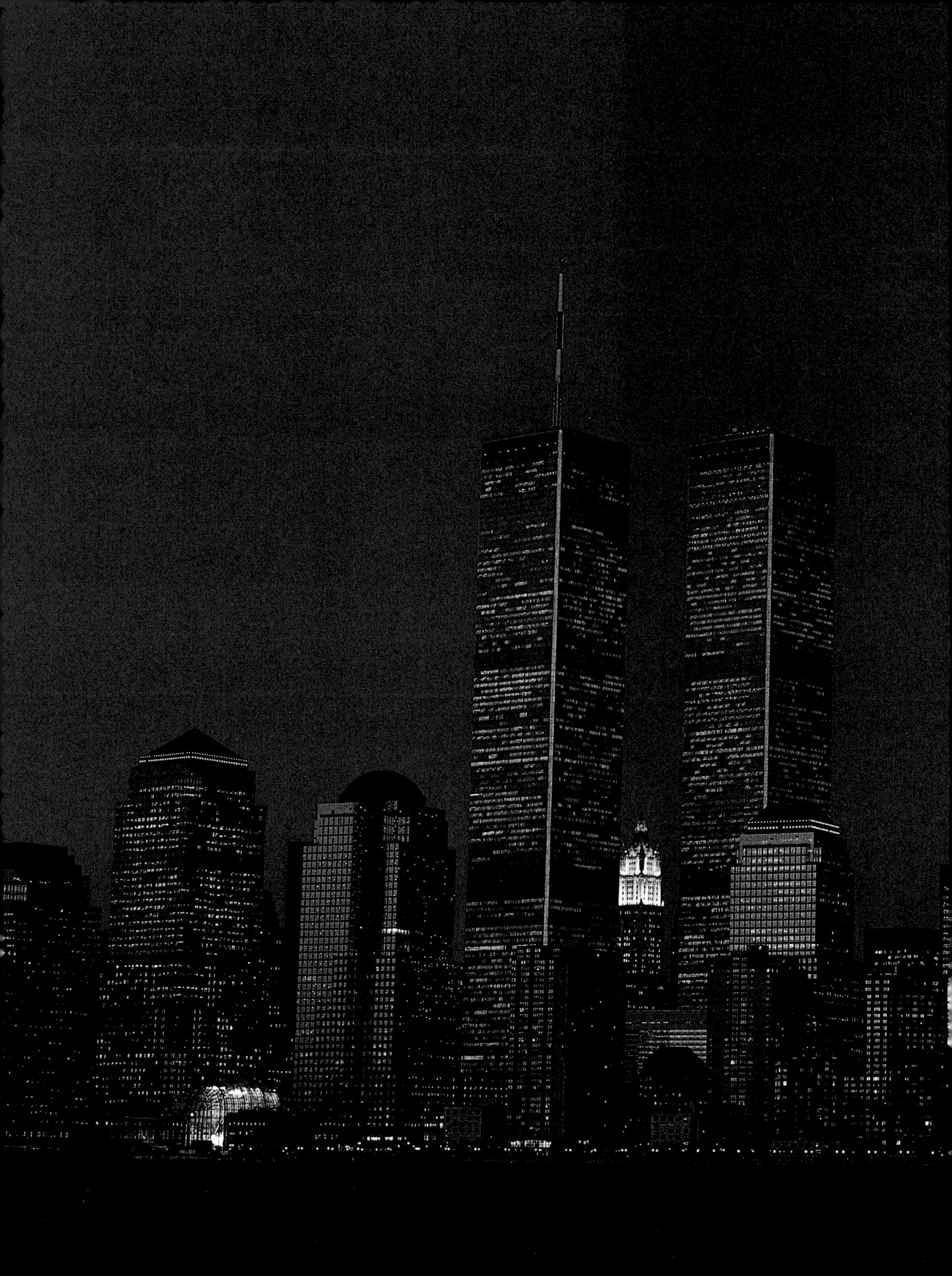

and commercial importance to match. But in its variety, dynamism, productivity, and richness of display, New York City is without peer; it is simply inexhaustible.

From the very beginning, New York had extraordinary resources to build upon. When the Dutch explorer Henry Hudson first sailed into the bay in 1609 and navigated north on the river now named for him, he marveled at the vast and tranquil natural harbor, ideally situated for trade up and down the coast. Hardwood forests blanketed the far landscape. The waters teemed with fish life. One important asset was hidden from Hudson's appraising eye, however: Manhattan Island's stratum of firm bedrock—called Manhattan schist—which in centuries to come would support buildings of almost limitless height.

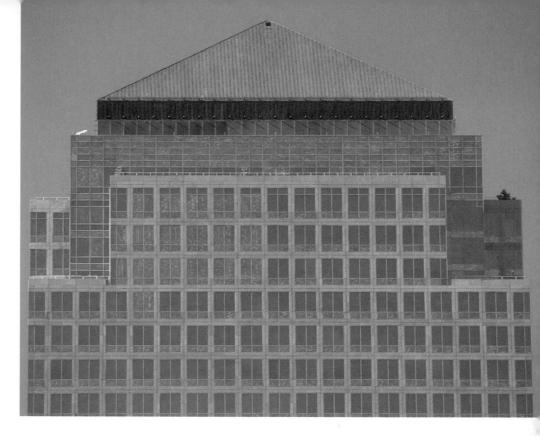

This page and opposite: *Buildings of the World Financial Center occupy landfill excavated in construction of the World Trade Center (seen towering behind them). Amenities of the new center include a large boat basin and a glass-enclosed Winter Garden. Preceding pages: New Jerseyites enjoy this view of Lower Manhattan, seen here at twilight.*

Left: *A sense of history pervades the Wall Street area, heart of New York's financial district. George Washington fêted his officers at Fraunces Tavern (this building is a reconstruction of the original).* Below: *He was sworn in as President at the spot where a statue of him now stands, in front of Federal Hall on Wall Street.* Opposite: *An island of calm—Trinity Church Cemetery at the head of Wall Street. New York Stock Exchange presents a dignified exterior, but inside, trading is frantic.*

A thumbnail sketch of New York City's growth begins in 1624 with the arrival of Dutch and Walloon families sent by the Dutch West India Company. Nieuw Amsterdam was the name chosen for their settlement in lower Manhattan. When England, a trading rival, wrested control of the island from the Dutch in 1664, they changed its name to New York. Nine years later the Dutch recaptured the island and christened it New Orange. Their dominance ended only a year later, however, when the Treaty of Westminster established New York as British. And so it remained until 1783 when the British Army, vanquished in the War of Independence, took to their ships and left for good.

Immigrant groups began arriving early. Among the first was a group of 23 Jews fleeing persecution in Brazil, who settled here in 1654. The 1700s was not a period of rapid population increase. But that changed suddenly in the last decade of the 18th century, when the census count for Manhattan Island almost doubled; in 1800, 60,515 persons were counted. From this point the pace of immigration continued to quicken, spurred by the potato famine that struck Ireland in 1846 and by political unrest in Germany. By 1855 housing was so inadequate that a tenement reform movement was called for. The number of people in Manhattan passed the million mark between 1870 and 1880 and the 2 million mark between 1900 and 1910. As the city limits were expanded to include the boroughs (Brooklyn, the Bronx, Queens, and Staten Island), total population shot up, reaching 7.5 million just before World War II.

At the last official census in 1980, the population of Manhattan was counted as 1,428,285 and that of Greater New York as 7,071,639. From this huge and varied population, New York derives its remarkable vitality and rich texture, endlessly interesting to residents and visitors alike.

This page: *An even more startling contrast pits the graceful dome of City Hall against the neo-Gothic shaft of the Woolworth Building and, behind it, the monolithic towers of the World Trade Center. Opposite: Trinity Church was the third to be built on this site for a parish founded in 1697. Richard Upjohn's design, a Gothic in brownstone, was built in 1846. Its 280-foot spire remains impressive, even amid the skyscrapers that surround it.*

New York resembles other cities in that it is arranged informally into districts and neighborhoods, areas where people of like interests, occupations, and cultural backgrounds cluster together. Now and then a district vanishes as commercial buildings are turned to residential or corporate use, but, surprisingly, many of New York City's old districts still survive.

Most famous, perhaps, is the financial district, near the southern tip of Manhattan. "Wall Street" is the shorthand term for this area of banks, brokerage houses, and stock and commodity exchanges. First-time visitors here often are surprised to find that "the Street," known the world over as the symbol of the capitalist system, is in fact a fairly narrow thoroughfare, not much wider than an alley.

A magnet for most visitors to New York is "Broadway," by which we mean the theater district on the west side of midtown (street numbers in the 40s and 50s). While a few new theaters have been built here and more are planned, most of the theaters date back to an era of ornate interior design, with plush seats and intricate plasterwork picked out with gold leaf. Decades of unforgettable

This page and opposite: *The World Trade Center: Its six buildings house agencies, offices, and banks dealing in international commerce. Since their completion in 1977, the Twin Towers, 1,350 feet tall, dominate the New York City skyline. Artworks in the five-acre plaza, like Fritz Koenig's bronze* Globe, *are suitably monumental in scale.*

performances have enshrined these playhouses in theatrical history, but there is nothing fusty about them. This is still the place to come to see the newest hits and the ageless classics. And for playwrights, directors, actors, and actresses everywhere, Broadway is still the pinnacle they strive for.

Not many blocks south of the theater district lies the garment district, or "Seventh Avenue" in the parlance of the fashion industry. It's a scene enlivened by deliverymen unloading bolts of cloth, by runners pushing pipe racks laden with new clothes. It may be hard to believe, but what we wear is largely decided for us in the work rooms and at the drawing boards of Seventh Avenue designers. Will our trousers be pegged or loose? Our waists cinched or bloused? Our skirts long or short? A peek at the garments on the pipe racks might tell, but they are chastly shrouded and the runners move them along at a rattling good pace. Stagnation is anathema to Seventh Avenue—its world begins anew with each turn of the season, with each new collection.

This page: *On the other side of Manhattan, New York's maritime past lives on at the South Street Seaport Museum, where old-time vessels are on view. Seaport visitors can stroll, shop, and admire the Brooklyn Bridge. The Fulton Fish Market has been in business here since the 1820s.* Opposite: *Glass-enclosed Winter Garden of the World Financial Center is a magnificent new addition to the downtown scene.*

Diagonally across town from the garment district—on the Upper East Side—is an area, actually a voting district, known as "the Silk Stocking District." The common thread in these largely residential blocks is "old money" salted with plenty of new. Upper Park Avenue is the main artery here, and several times a year the mall dividing north- and southbound traffic is replanted with flowers and shrubs—or festooned with Christmas lights—as the season dictates. The sidewalks here are broad, the building lobbies have cadres of uniformed doormen, and the apartments seem to go on forever. The Silk Stocking District may not be rife with visual excitement, but there is the occasional visual joke to add interest: the aging Volkswagen parked at the curb bearing a four-letter license plate—MAID; the professional dog-walker sailing along amid an armada of bobbing tails—a dozen or more dogs, large and small, all on their best behavior.

This page: *The Brooklyn Bridge is a poem in granite and steel. One hundred years old in 1983, its beauty remains inspiring.* Opposite: *Besides its East River piers, the South Street Historic District includes five blocks of late-18th- and early 19th-century buildings. Many have been restored to exhibit crafts and trades from the age of sail.* Overleaf: *East River traffic passing beneath the effortless span of the Brooklyn Bridge.*

Above: *Clothing shops on the Lower East Side's Orchard Street, a magnet for bargain hunters.* Below: *Food stall at the colorful San Gennaro festival, a mid-September event in Little Italy.*

New York City's Upper East Side also has a concentration of galleries dealing in the works of the world's major artists and artisans. The "gallery district" is roughly from 57th Street to the lower 80s, with Madison Avenue as its axis. Paintings and sculpture can, of course, be viewed and purchased, but even more fascinating is the plethora of antique silver, porcelain, glassware, furniture, hand-woven rugs, and jewelry, displayed in windows fronting the sidewalks.

Left: Firecrackers and fearsome "dragons" ring in the Chinese New Year. Below: Building in Chinatown with tiled roof and curving eaves, traditional features of Chinese architecture.

In the evening, these well-lighted windows can be studied at leisure. This is truly New York's "museum without walls." Only an eager eye is needed to take it all in.

The Manhattan waterfront has all the ingredients of a district: a locality and a network of occupations—from longshoremen to tug boat crews to ship's captains to harbor pilots—all in the service of shipping. Sadly, in recent years the industry has taken most of its business elsewhere, to New Jersey ports in particular. Only a few of the mighty ocean liners still call here, mostly as cruise ships, and they berth at the New York City Passenger Terminal, a modern facility on the Hudson River between 48th and 52nd streets. Elsewhere along the shoreline the neo-Gothic-style piers built in the golden age of transatlantic travel are falling into decay. Still, there are those evenings when the *Queen Elizabeth II* heads out to sea, her every deck atwinkle with lights, the sound of her orchestra wafting faintly over the water, when the onlooker realizes that here is an elegance of form and a vestige of Old World standards rarely seen these days.

These are but a sampling of New York City's districts; there are many more—districts for diamond merchants, florists, milliners, photographers, pornographers, meat packers, fish mongers, butter-and-egg men. Whatever one's livelihood or interest, there is undoubtedly a place in New York City where others of like mind have gathered.

This page: *Classical motifs in various guises. A lanterned pyramid tops the mid-1920s Con Ed Building, while open prisms cap newer residential buildings in the foreground. Triumphal arch is the formal entryway to Washington Square Park. Opposite: At 23rd Street, the superb Flatiron Building marks the acute-angle intersection of Broadway and Fifth Avenue (center).*

There is really no way to equip oneself for the experience of New York, except perhaps with the gift of tongues. All the world seems to be here—people from Africa, Asia, Europe, Central and South America, India. They, too, have their neighborhoods, identified by the accents and cuisines special to each group. Guidebooks to New York never fail to point out Chinatown and Little Italy on the Lower East Side; Greenwich Village, with its artists and writers; and Harlem, a large area north of 96th Street now shared largely by African-American and Hispanic groups. But besides these places, there are mini-neighborhoods sprinkled all over the city. You can buy an Indian sari on Lexington Avenue in the lower 30s, Portuguese goods on 46th Street west of Fifth Avenue, German-style sausages in the east 80s area called Yorkville.

This page and opposite: Tower of Metropolitan Life Building (1909) was inspired by the campanile in the Piazza San Marco in Venice. It was the world's tallest building, a title later enjoyed for a while by the Empire State Building (background). Macy's, the world's largest store, wins friends young and old with its annual Thanksgiving Day Parade.

This page and opposite: *The Empire State Building, 102 stories, built in 19 months early in the Depression. While it fizzled as a mooring station for dirigibles, it stood steadfast when struck by a U.S. Army bomber in 1945. Its 16-story spire serves as an observation platform and transmission tower. Colors of top lighting honor the holiday of the moment. Twilight portrait here was taken on St. Patrick's Day. Overleaf: West Side skyline and piers, with carrier* Intrepid *at her West 46th Street berth.*

There are Greek tavernas in Queens and Russian chess clubs in Brooklyn. In the blocks northeast of Pennsylvania Station, Korean is the dominant language of shop signs. And the mix is made even more complex by cultural crossover—as on the Upper West Side, where simple restaurants typically advertise "Cuban-Chinese" cuisine.

Considering once again the size of Manhattan Island—a mere 22 square miles—the number of its world-famous structures and internationally respected institutions is astonishing.

Pride of place must go to the Statue of Liberty, given by the people of France and dedicated in 1886. The sight of Liberty, standing on a small island in the upper bay, her torch reaching 305 feet above sea level, lifts the hearts of all who come here.

Top to bottom: *The Intrepid Sea-Air-Space Museum welcomes visitors to the aircraft carrier's permanent mooring on the Hudson River. Jacob K. Javits Convention Center, overlooking the Hudson between 34th and 39th streets, opened in 1987. The ultramodern building uses natural light and the city skyline as a unique backdrop. The heart of the theater district, West 44th Street, where Sardi's Restaurant and several venerable playhouses make a star lineup.* Opposite: *Broadway, "the Great White Way," looking north from Times Square.*

Past this gateway rise the towers of Lower Manhattan, dominated by the stupendous twin skyscrapers of the World Trade Center, each 110 stories high with an acre of office space per floor. The observation deck of Tower Two (107th floor) is the place to see New York for what it truly is—one of the great port cities in the world, a city at the edge of the sea.

Liberty's only rival as the symbol of New York is the Empire State Building, at 34th Street and Fifth Avenue. Its exterior is somewhat somber, expressive of the determination that brought this 102-story building to completion in a mere nineteen months. Restrained Art Deco details soften its classically organized base and shaft. A sixteen-story observation tower completes the ensemble and rewards visitors with breath-taking views of the city.

A near neighbor at 42nd Street and Lexington Avenue, is the Chrysler Building, completed in 1930. The most extraordinary feature of this building is its stainless-steel spire, a complicated play of arches and

Top to bottom: *Even at Christmas, with ribbons and wreaths around their necks, the Library's stone lions retain their lordly demeanor. Snow bedecks terrace of the New York Public Library as Fifth Avenue traffic bustles by. Information booth in Main Concourse of Grand Central Terminal is an unfailing source of guidance for travelers. Opposite: South-facing façade of Grand Central Terminal is one of New York's handsomest essays in the Beaux-Arts style. Pan Am Building rises in background.*

triangles that seem to pierce the sky. Inside, the splendid lobby has walls clad in richly patterned African marble, and elevator doors of richly inlaid wood that rank as artworks in themselves.

On the blocks west of the Chrysler Building, Grand Central Terminal shelters a city within a city. Its subterranean levels conceal railway tracks and converging subway systems. At street level is the Main Concourse, a space of immense scale and dignity, with a vaulted ceiling painted to resemble the starry night sky. The south-facing façade is a powerful composition of columns, windows, and statuary in the Beaux-Arts style. One can only feel thankful to the architects of grand Central Terminal for somehow ennobling the mundane matter of getting from here to there.

Another of New York's favorite buildings is the Citicorp Center, at 53rd Street and Lexington Avenue, which opened in 1977. With its roofline canted at a 45-degree angle, and the color of its glass-and-aluminum walls changing subtly in different lights, it is one of the outstanding elements in the New York City skyline. There is an

Top to bottom: *Bronze statue in the U.N. Gardens, titled "Let Us Beat Our Swords Into Plowshares," was a gift of the USSR. Secretariat Building measures 544 feet high, 72 feet thick. United Nations buildings include Secretariat (left), Conference Building (bottom left), and General Assembly (bottom right). Skyscraper clad in green-tinted glass is One United Nations Plaza, a hotel and office building.* Opposite: *Tower of the Chrysler Building.*

Above: *Views of St. Patrick's Cathedral: Lady Chapel reflected in window of Villard House (now part of the Helmsley Palace Hotel); nave lighted for Christmas service; Gothic windows of the Lady Chapel.* Below: *Fifth Avenue façade, with Saks in foreground.* Opposite: *Spires of the Chrysler Building and Empire State Building.*

atmosphere of amenity in the Citicorp public spaces: in the three-story tree-planted atrium where there are tables for reading, snacking, and listening to live music; in the convenient and varied restaurants; in the colorful and sophisticated shops; in the outdoor sunken plaza, a sheltered place to lunch *al fresco*; in the prayerful quiet of St. Peter's Lutheran Church, which occupies the northwest corner of the site; even—wonder of wonders—in the well-tended rest rooms. Of the many so-called atrium buildings put up since the 1970s, perhaps none succeeds as well as Citicorp in luring and pleasing the public.

Dark glass façade of Olympic Tower on block north of St. Patrick's Cathedral contrasts with the church's Gothic tracery. Details of Main Portal of St. Patrick's: Rose window (26 feet in diameter), and frieze of Christ and Apostles above the bronze doors.

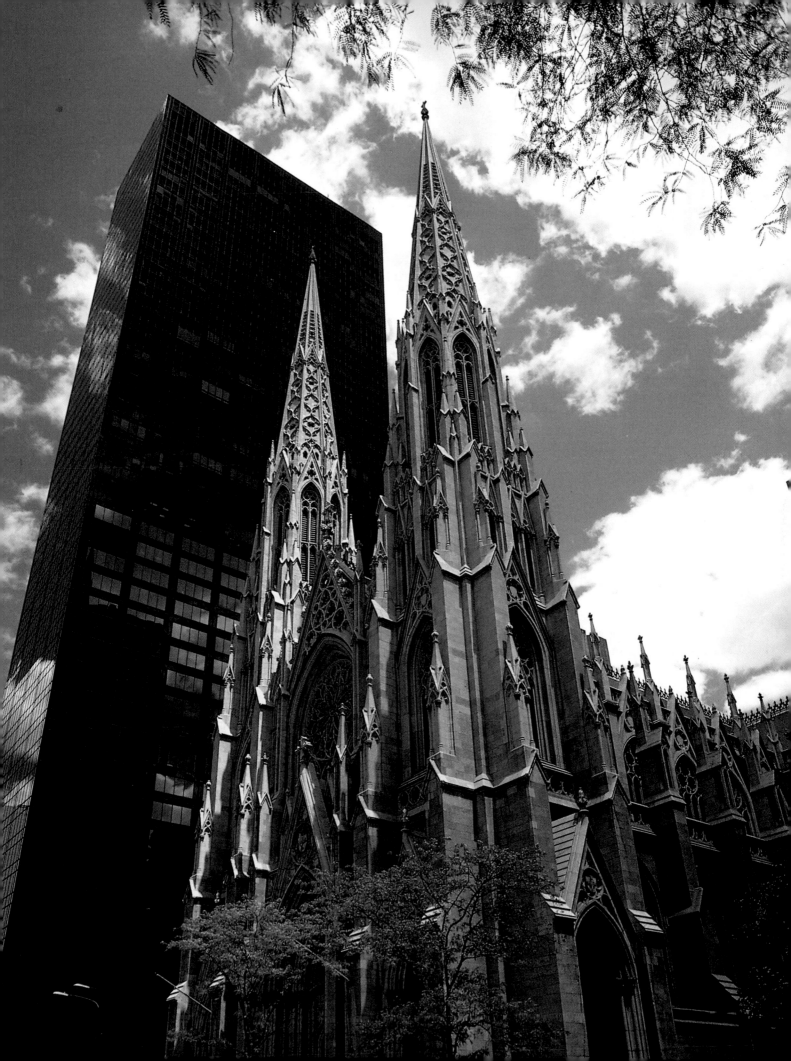

Above: *Rockefeller Center: Statue of Atlas, by Lee Lawrie, facing St. Patrick's Cathedral. Lawrie's relief "Genius," over the east entrance of the General Electric Building (formerly RCA Building). Atlas (front view) at Fifth Avenue entrance to the International Building.* Below: *Statue of Prometheus overlooking the sunken plaza.* Opposite: *Promenade, or "Channel Gardens," leads the visitor down a gentle incline toward the majestic centerpiece of Rockefeller Center, the GE Building.*

This page and opposite: *Holiday time at Rockefeller Center: Skaters skim the ice, angels herald the joy of the season, and the Christmas Tree—with its thousands of multicolored lights—illuminates the scene.*

Moving west from Citicorp, to Fifth Avenue between 49th and 51st streets, we come upon "an island of architectural excellence." This is how the American Institute of Architects, in its guidebook to New York City, describes Rockefeller Center. Perhaps the best-known feature of this group of buildings is the central Promenade that leads visitors down a gentle incline

This page and opposite: *More successful architecturally is the recently enlarged Museum of Modern Art on West 53rd Street, where artworks and fountains mingle in the Sculpture Garden. Corporate headquarters buildings west of Sixth Avenue (Exxon and McGraw-Hill, for example) are considered part of an "enlarged" Rockefeller Center. Radio City Music Hall at Rockefeller Center offers exuberant stage shows featuring the Rockettes, a corps of high-stepping precision dancers. Patrons get to see the theater's sumptuous Art Deco furnishings and decor.*

toward a sunken plaza and a gilded statue of Prometheus. The buildings charm with their wealth of decorative details— murals, reliefs, statuary—but more fundamental to their success is their varying scale, their relationship to one another, and their beautiful finish, inside and out. Surely one of the most joyous sights in the city is the Promenade and Plaza here, with their streaming fountains, floral displays, fluttering flags, and ice skating rink (set for outdoor dining in the summer). The theatrical showpiece among these buildings is Radio City Music Hall, a veritable temple of 1930s Art Deco design.

Farther up the avenue, the Metropolitan Museum of Art houses collections so extensive and important that the visitor almost blinks in disbelief. Wall after wall of master paintings, galleries filled with exquisite ceramics and priceless antiquities, rooms of period furniture: the Met, like the city itself, is inexhaustible. To protect and display all this, several wings and additions have been built over the years; nothing however rivals the Renaissance-style Fifth Avenue façade and the lofty room that greets you as you pass through the doors, a fitting introduction to 5,000 years of great art.

Almost directly west of the Metropolitan, on the other side of Central Park, is the American Museum of Natural History, four stories of connected buildings in different architectural styles. The museum covers four city blocks, and is chock full of fascinating exhibits, including a 66-foot *Brontosaurus* skeleton;

This page and opposite: *Two buildings instantly recognizable by their rooflines: Citicorp Center has glass-and-aluminum walls and terminates in an eye-catching 45-degree angle, while AT&T's new skyscraper headquarters has pink granite facing and an open-pediment top. Citicorp's sloping roof has yet to be used for its intended purpose—as a solar collector.*

incredibly lifelike dioramas showing birds and mammals in their natural habitats, and others showing peoples of early cultures with their tools, weapons, and ornaments; a Hall of Gems with many superior specimens on display; and, in the astronomy wing (Hayden Planetarium), an ingeniously projected model of the solar system.

What the Metropolitan Museum is to art and the Natural History Museum is to nature, the New York Public Library Main Branch (42nd Street and Fifth Avenue) is to the written word. Its rich collections of books, manuscripts, prints, and maps place it second only to the Library of Congress. The building itself is one of New York's most beautiful examples of the Beaux-Arts style, providing monumental and inspiring spaces where the public can come in the pursuit of knowledge.

Six blocks east of the library, ideally located on the East River, is the Headquarters of the United Nations, an organization dedicated to the pursuit of world peace. Visiting the U.N. is like visiting another country; indeed, the eighteen-acre site actually has a separate territorial status.

This page and opposite: *Gucci and Bergdorf's, Cartier and Tiffany's are just a few of the stores that make Fifth Avenue the most famous shopping street in the world. Also on Fifth, the six-story atrium of Trump Tower dazzles with its interplay of rich marble, polished metal, and ingenious lighting. The distinctively stepped façade of Trump Tower.*

This page: *Flags whipping in the breeze surmount the entrance to The Plaza, the grandest of New York's grand hotels. Guests enjoy attentive service and a view of Central Park.*

Four buildings house various activities: the Library, the Conference Building, the General Assembly, and the slab-shaped Secretariat looming above them in gleaming isolation. The U.N. welcomes visitors: you can take a tour, attend a meeting, lunch in the Delegates' Dining Room, even view major artworks donated by the member nations.

New York's great buildings and institutions are only the beginning of the city's cultural riches. Among the many other important museums displaying the fine arts are the Asia House, the Brooklyn Museum, the Cloisters (a branch of the Metropolitan Museum devoted to medieval art), the Frick Collection, the Pierpont Morgan Library, and—for modern art— the Museum of Modern Art, the Guggenheim Museum, and the Whitney Museum. There are also museums devoted to the crafts, folk art, photography, history, even broadcasting.

But New York does not merely house and protect culture; its artists, writers, and performers make it a cultural fountainhead. Painters, sculptors, designers, and photographers find inspiration and an interested audience here. Bestselling books are born here. For aspiring performers, there are schools and teachers of acting, singing, and dancing.

Top to bottom: *Not far away stands Carnegie Hall. The blocky brown-brick building, famous for its acoustics and revered in musical history, was nearly demolished in the 1960s. Lincoln Center includes buildings specially designed for ballet, opera, symphony, and theater presentations. The Metropolitan Opera House, with its five tall arches, is neighbor to Avery Fisher Hall on the Plaza.*

The West Side has many buildings from an earlier age of opulence. In 1904, the Ansonia Hotel, at Broadway and
73rd Street, reproduced the splendors of a Parisian palais, with balconies, cupolas, and a mansard roof. Original
main entrance of the American Museum of Natural History, on West 77th Street, is a Romanesque Revival
composition with turrets, curving staircase, and porte-cochère.

Theater-goers have more choices than they can keep up with. Nightclubs, cabarets, piano bars, humor clubs, discos pulsate through the night. There are countless movie houses showing art films, blockbusters, and revivals. The great symphony orchestras of the world—including New York's own—play at Avery Fisher Hall and at the acoustically superb Carnegie Hall.

The avant-gardes of music, dance, and opera have a home in the Brooklyn Academy of Music. Two opera companies, housed side-by-side on the Plaza at Lincoln Center, mount opera productions in the grand manner. Also at Lincoln Center—as well as at the City Center Theater and in smaller spaces throughout the city—celebrated dance companies can be seen almost any night of the year. New York's institutions of higher learning—led by Columbia University and New York University—each year graduate a new crop of writers, scientists, teachers, theologians, MBAs. Each year, too, startling and controversial buildings, the works of leading architects, arise with astonishing speed and remarkably little construction mess. And if cuisine is a measure of civilization, New York is highly civilized, for it has many chefs of genius whose dishes, both classical and innovative, can be sampled in a marvelous array of restaurants.

This page: *Two monuments on Riverside Drive are the tomb of Ulysses S. Grant and the more modest Soldiers' and Sailors' Monument commemorating Civil War dead.*

Above: *Interior views of the Metropolitan Museum of Art. Left, Garden Court in the American Wing, with a Greek Revival façade preserved from a 1826 bank building. Middle, the magnificent domed Main Hall. Right, exhibit of primitive art in the Rockefeller Wing. Below, monumental portal overlooking Fifth Avenue.*

This page: *Guggenheim Museum, where visitors view artworks while descending a spiral ramp. Completed in 1959, it is Frank Lloyd Wright's only building in New York City.*

New York can fulfill every shopper's desire. Designer labels sell at bargain prices on the Lower East Side and for sticker-shock sums in the stores on upper Fifth Avenue and in the boutiques on Madison Avenue. Tucked away on side streets are shops where talented freelance designers sell the clothing, jewelry, and leather goods they create. There are dealers in every kind of collectible—whether it's stamps, music boxes, or toy soldiers.

Not even New Yorkers can keep up with the city's beat every minute, though. They need times of rest and contemplation, and the city answers this need as well. There are churches small and large, from tiny Trinity Church at the head of Wall Street, to the Cathedral of St. John the Divine in Upper Manhattan, the largest Gothic-

style church in the world. St. Patrick's Cathedral, a neo-Gothic edifice on Fifth Avenue across from Rockefeller Center, is one of the city's most famous landmarks, and St. Bartholomew's, on Park Avenue at 51st Street, is one of its most remarkable-looking churches, mixing Byzantine and Romanesque elements. Whatever one's denomination or persuasion, there is a place in New York—a meditation center, chapel, church, or synagogue—in which to find spiritual refreshment.

A refuge of another sort stretches from 59th Street to 110th Street. Central Park's 840 acres preserve a sense of natural beauty artfully blended with many man-made features. There are lakes, fountains, bridges, bridle paths, tennis courts, skating rinks, a boat house, a croquet lawn, a band shell, and a Mall. There are playgrounds,

This page and opposite: *Three of Central Park's remarkable features. Belvedere Castle, on a 135-foot promontory called Vista Rock. Model Boathouse and Conservatory Water, a venue for toy-boat enthusiasts. Cleopatra's Needle, an obelisk dating to 1600 BC.*

playing fields, huge lawns, wooded copses, rocky crags. In May, the flowerbeds and blossoming trees and shrubs put on a wondrous display of color; in the snows of winter, the park is an oasis of quiet.

Perhaps nothing expresses the vitality of New York better than its parades and feasts. These start with a bang in January or February when Chinatown celebrates its New Year. The city's Irish march up Fifth Avenue on St. Patrick's Day in March, and in the ensuing months almost every other large national and ethnic group parades the same route. Then, too, there are the Easter Parade, the annual parade of circus animals to Madison Square Garden, and the Macy's Thanksgiving Day Parade.

Food fêtes start in May with the huge Ninth Avenue International Festival. The West Indian Festival takes place on Labor Day, the San Gennaro in mid-September in Little Italy. December brings the magical lighting of the Rockefeller Center Christmas Tree. Fireworks boom out over the city in the waning hours of December 31st. At 12:01 AM on January 1st, New York City opens the calendar on another superlative year.

This page: *Central Park: New Yorkers sunning on the Sheep Meadow. Mosaic in Strawberry Fields, the John Lennon memorial. Bow Bridge, glimpsed through summer greenery, with the Dakota, on Central Park West, visible in the background.* Opposite: *Another of the park's many graceful bridges.* Overleaf: *Skaters on Wollman Memorial Rink.*

Index of Photography

All photographs courtesy of The Image Bank,
except where indicated*